MW01625144

ST. FRANCIS PREACHES TO THE BIRDS

ST. FRANCIS PREACHES TO THE BIRDS

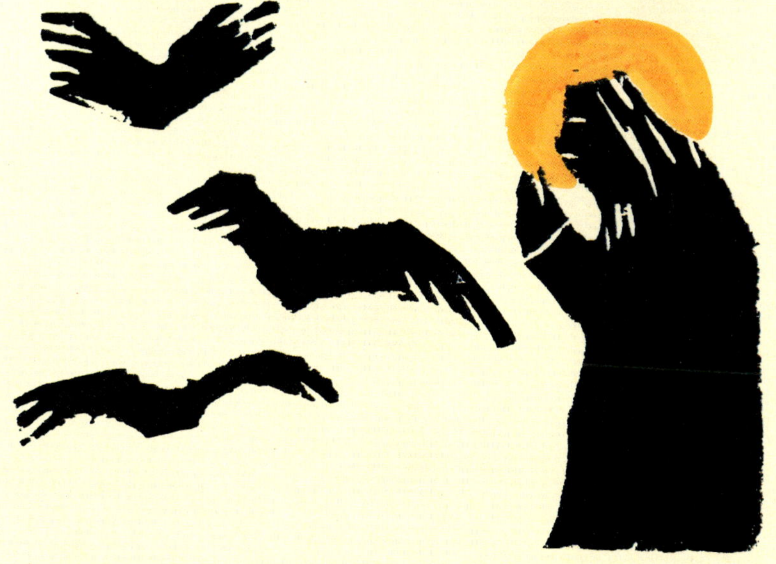

CHRONICLE BOOKS + SAN FRANCISCO

THIS IS ST. FRANCIS

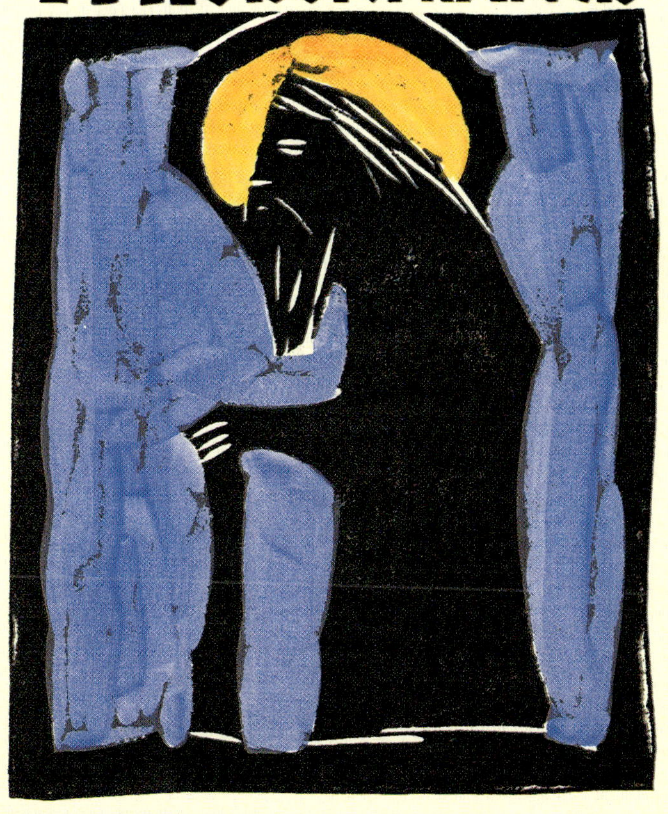

IT'S 5 A.M. WAKE UP ST. FRANCIS!

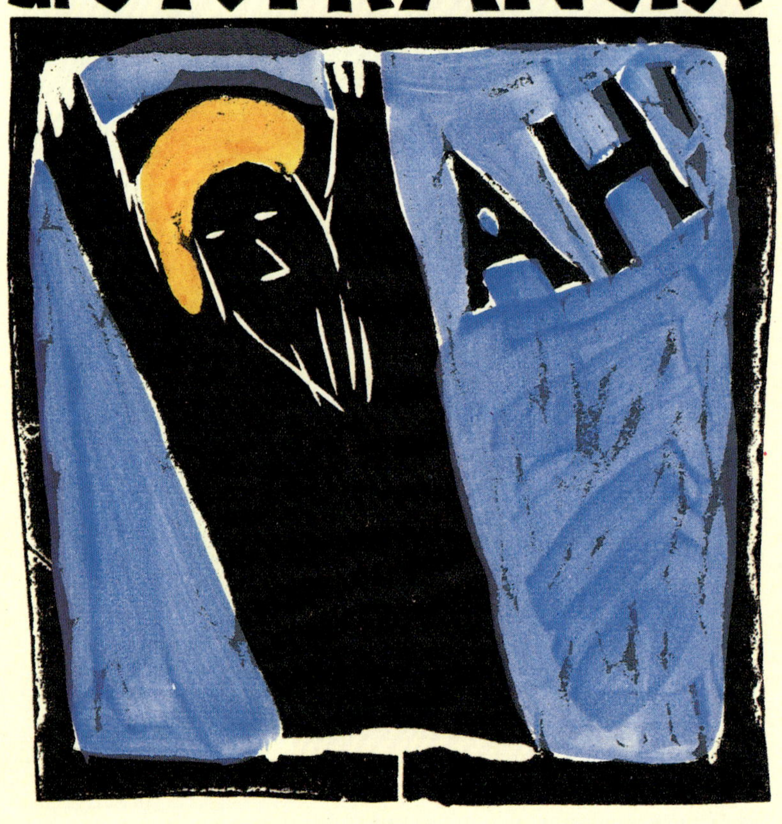

HE OPENS THE WINDOW & SINGS: TRA-LA-LA

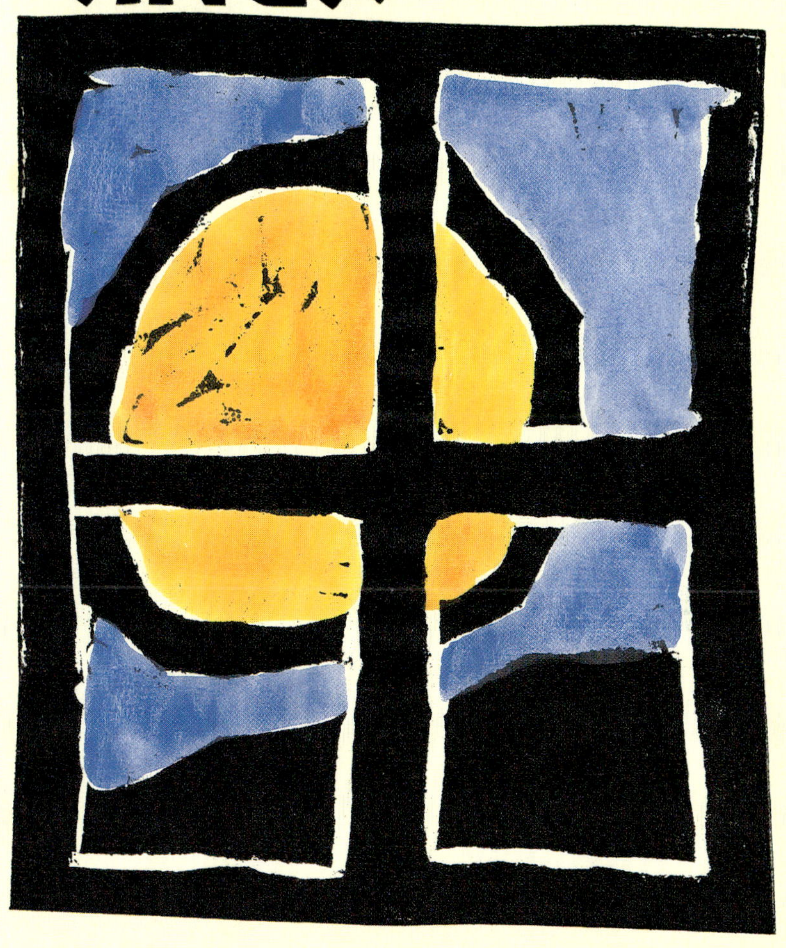

HE BRUSHES HIS TEETH &SAYS: THANK YOU TEETH!

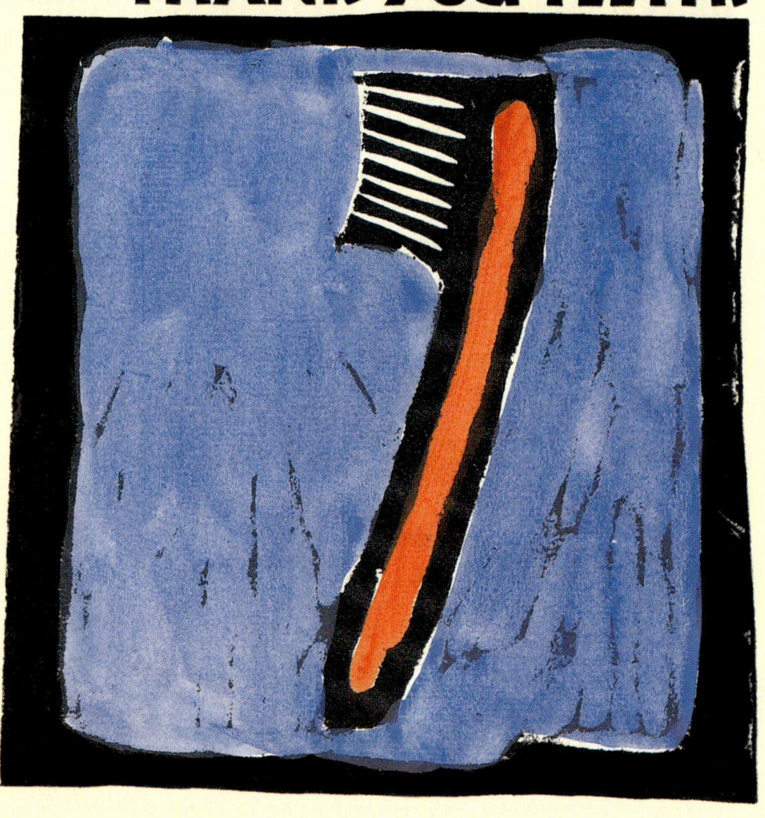

HE WASHES HIS TOES
& SAYS: THANK YOU TOES!

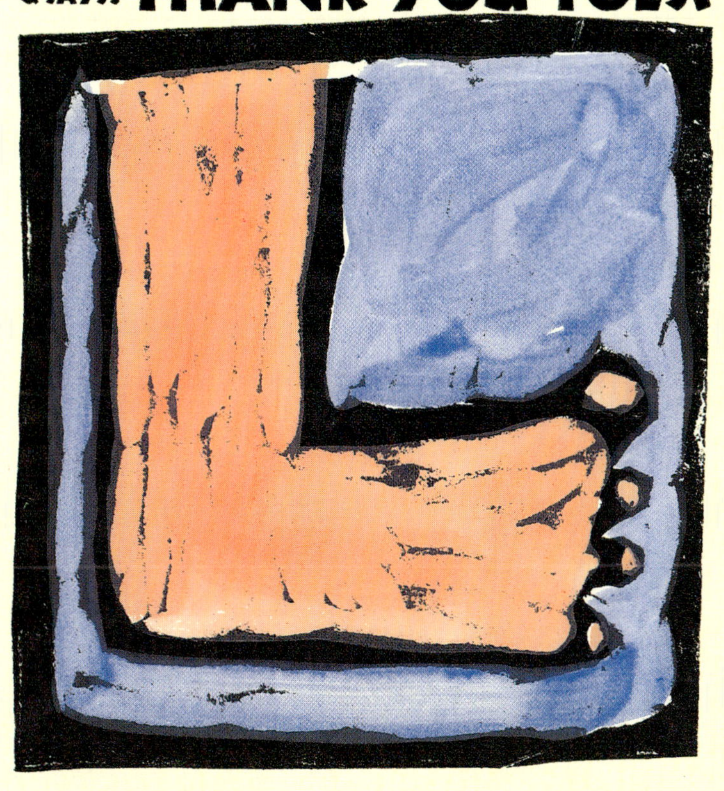

HE GETS MILK

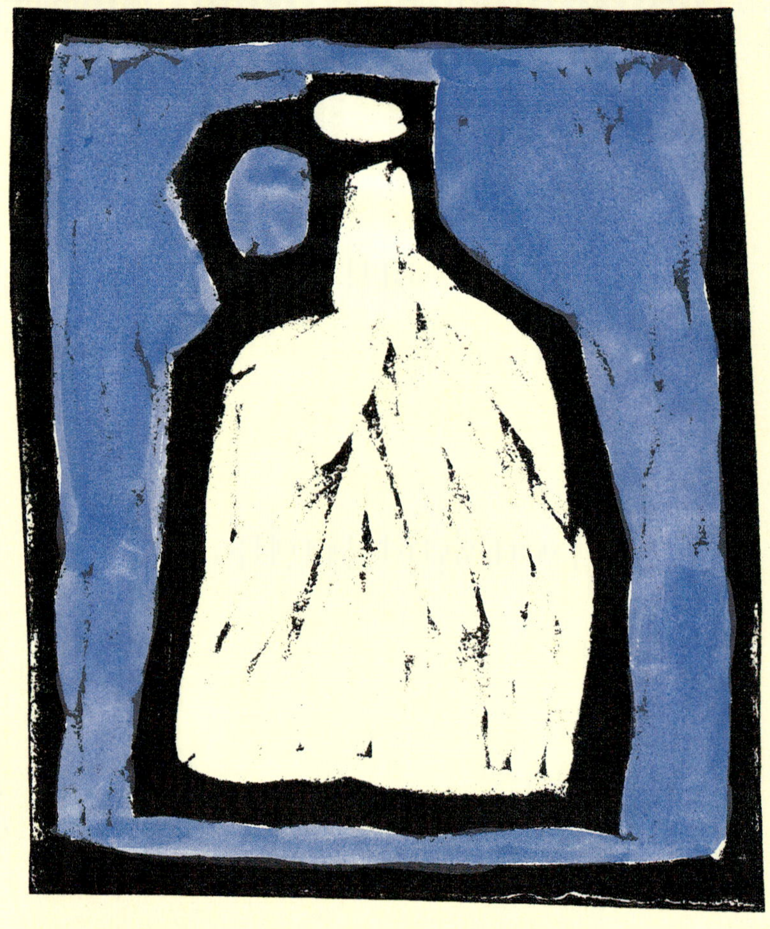

DRINKS HIS COFFEE & SAYS THANK YOU COFFEE!

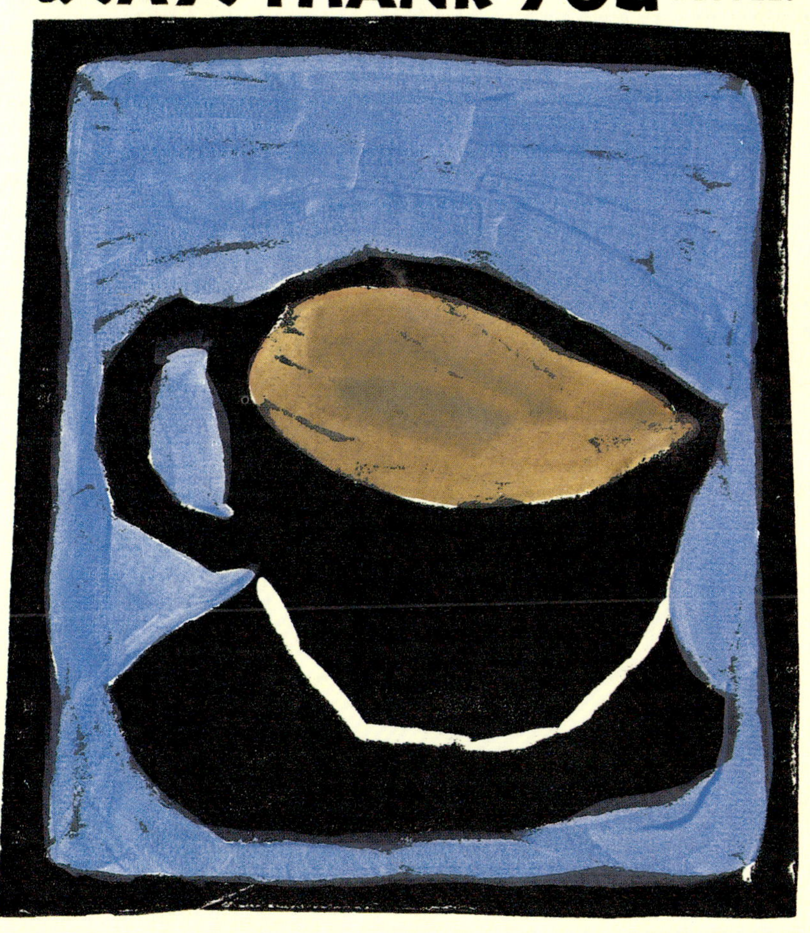

HE GOES THROUGH THE TOWN

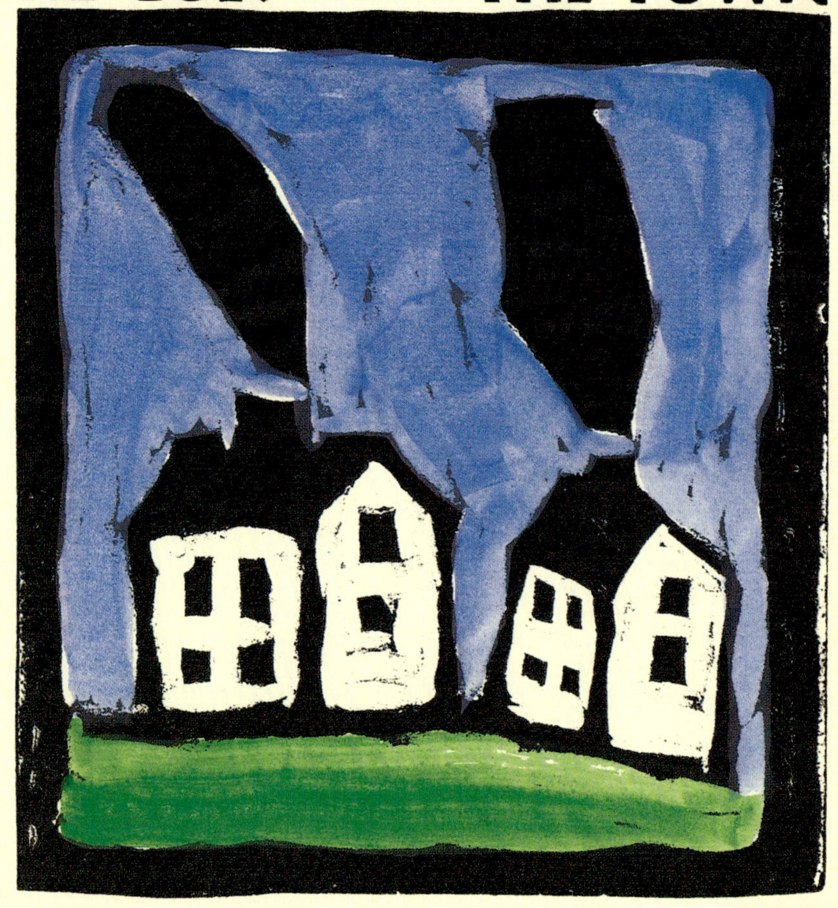

THROUGH THE APPLE ORCHARD

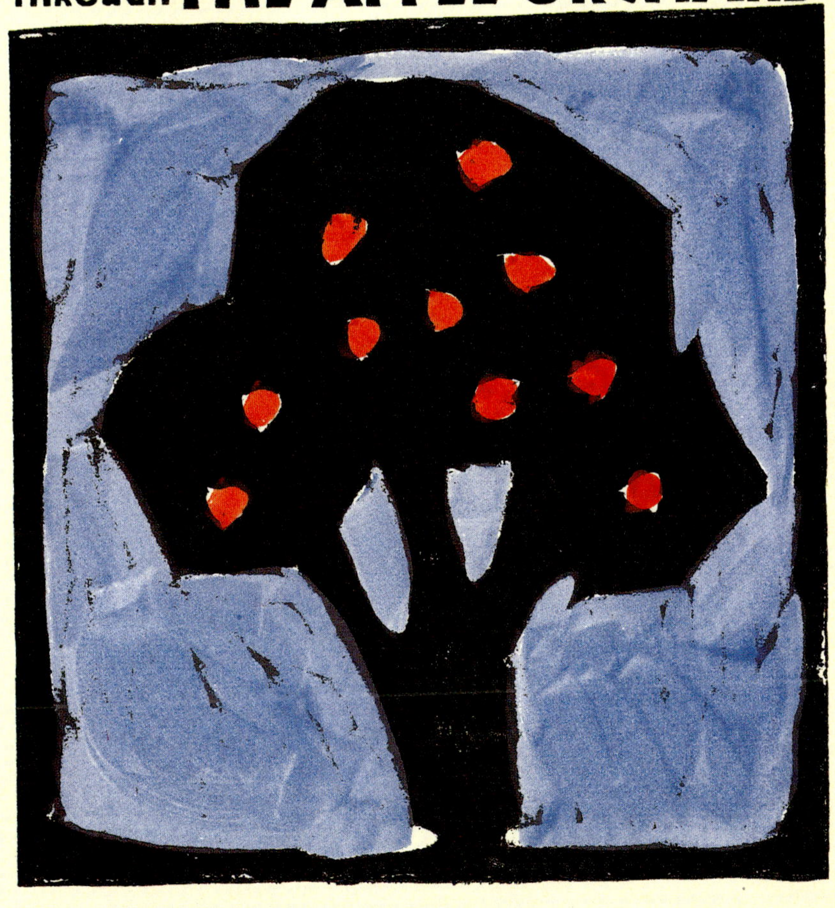

OVER THE PASTURE

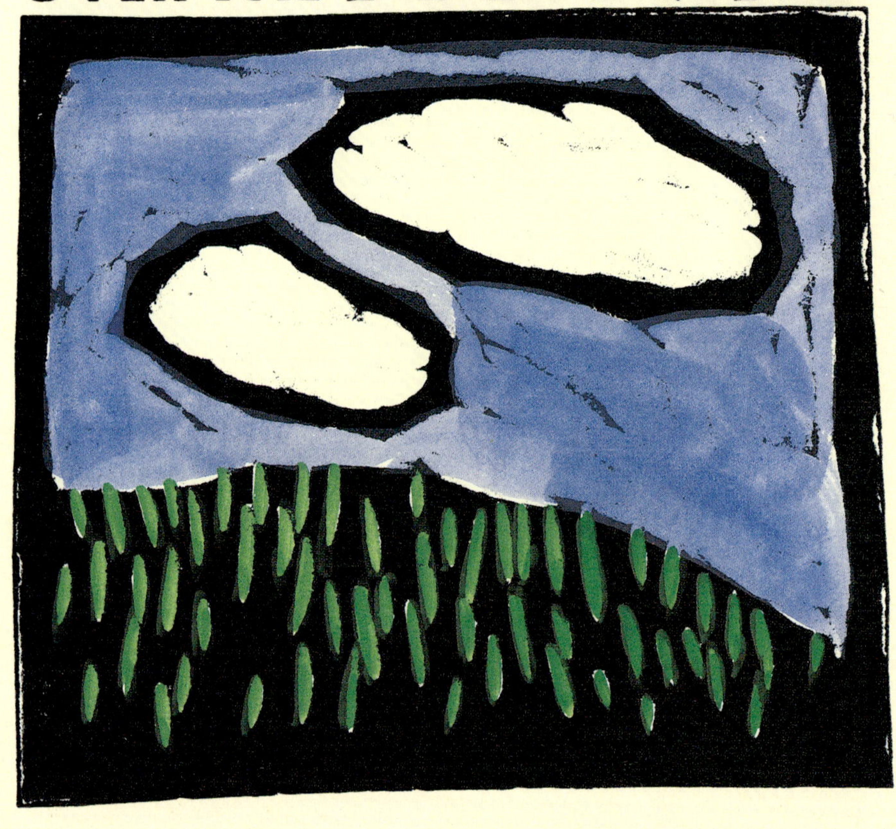

& UP THE HILL!

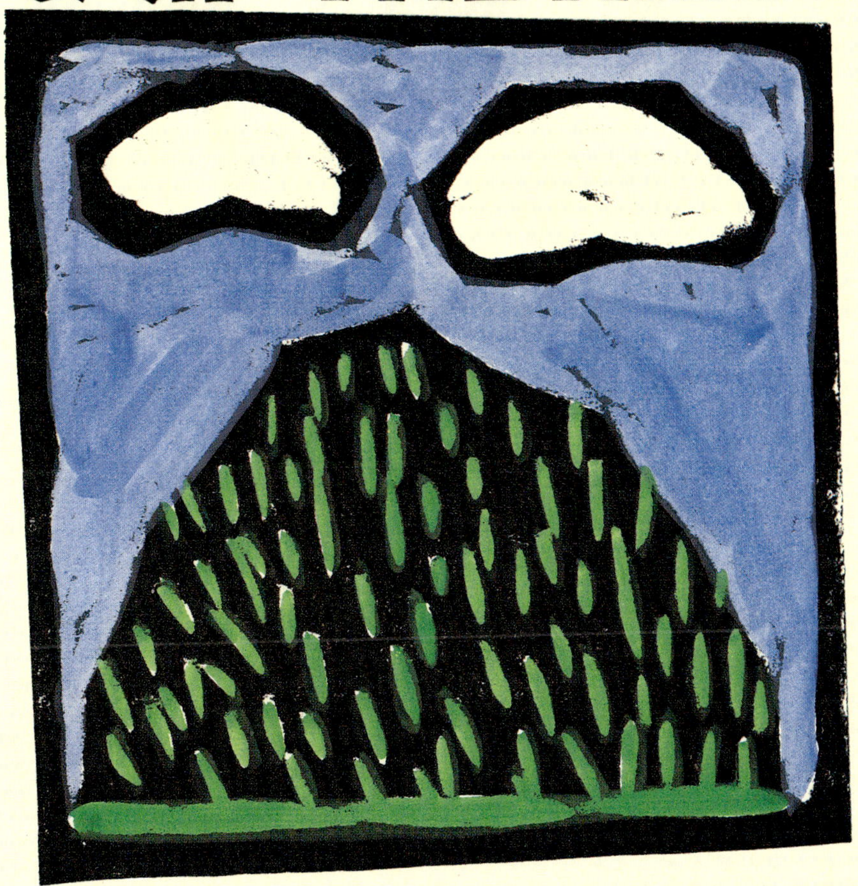

& THE BIRDS COME FLYING

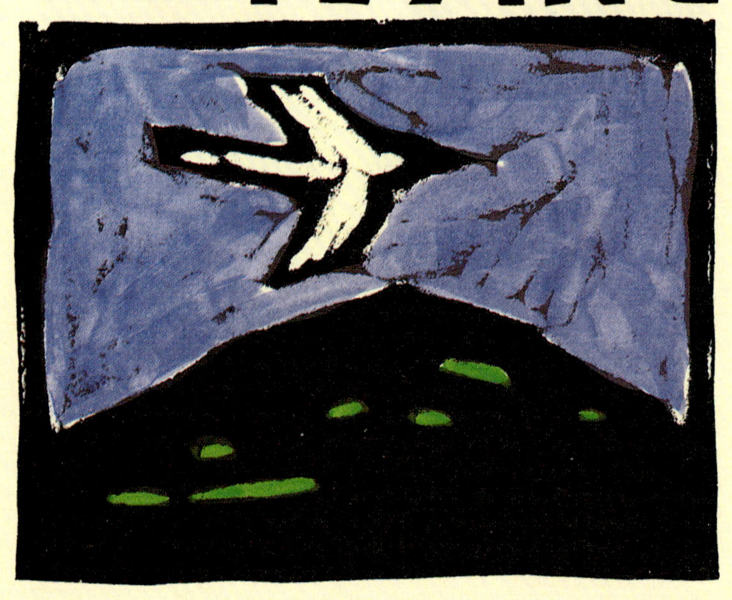

FLYING FLYING

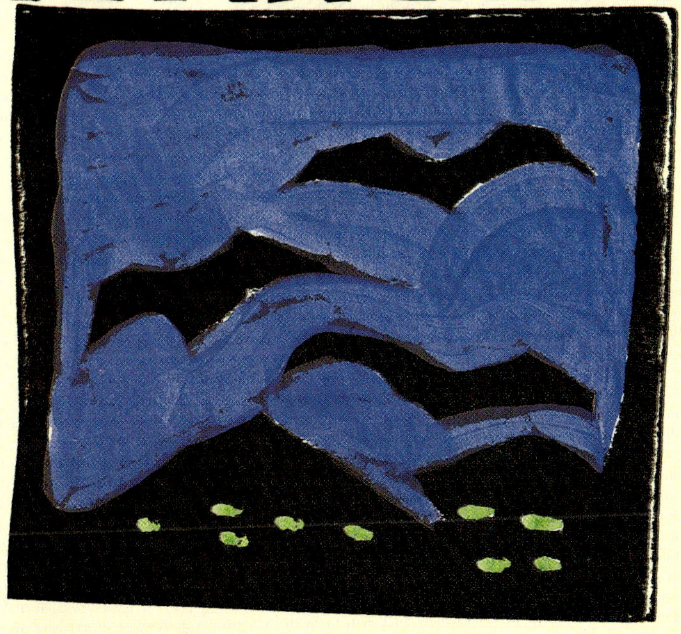

FLYING FLYING FLYING FLYING

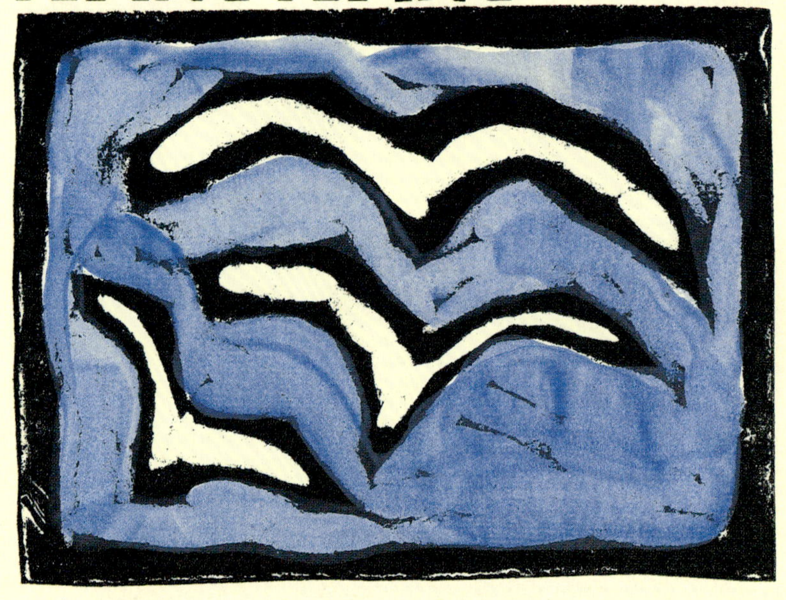

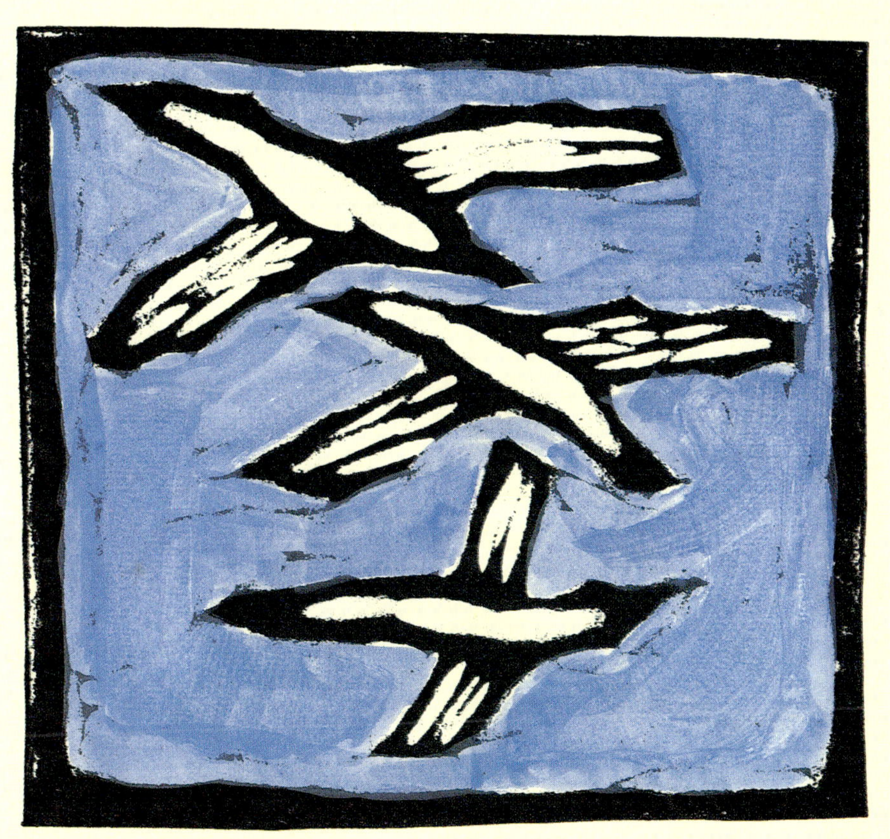

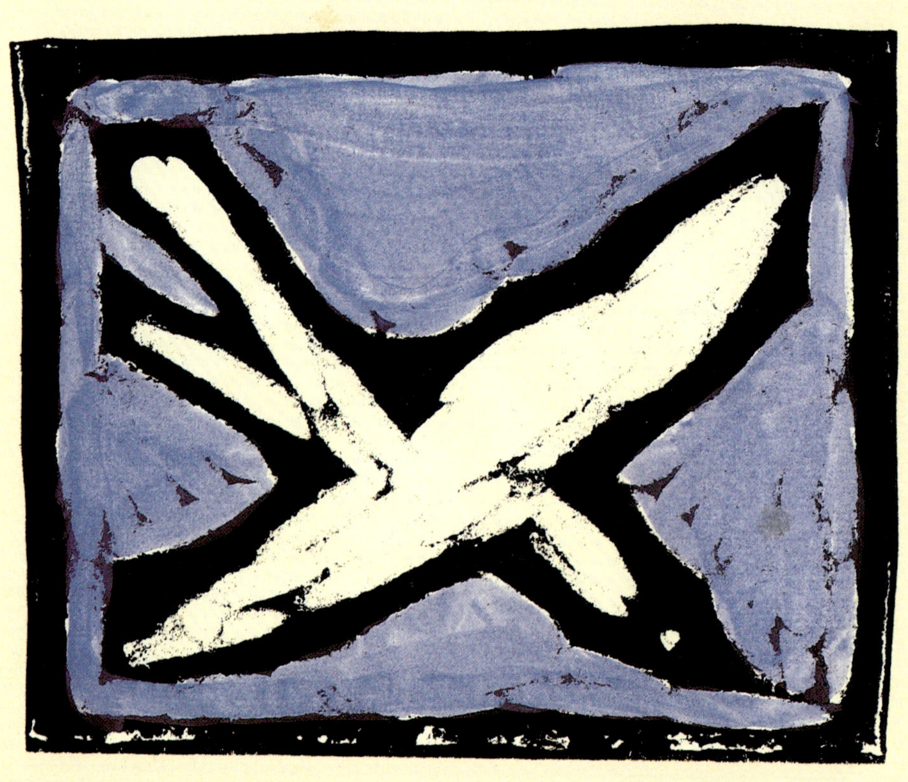

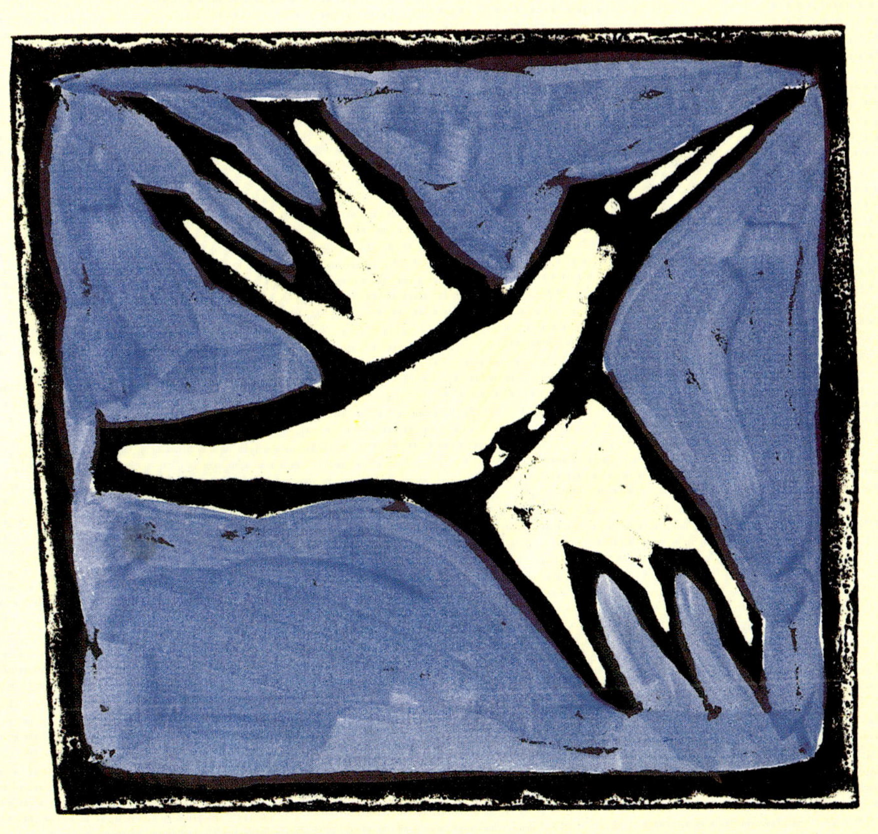

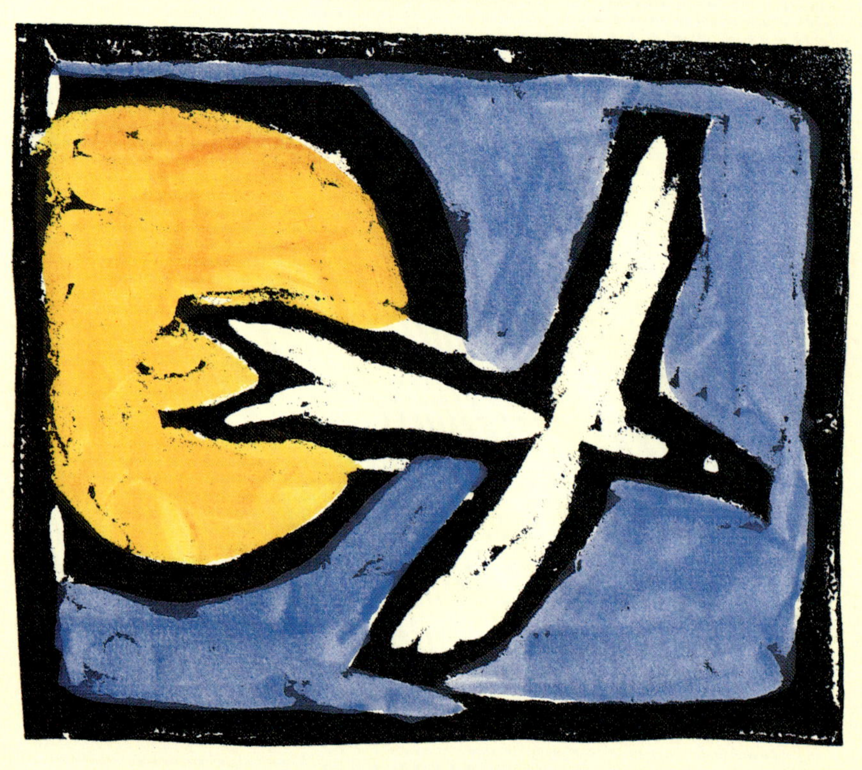

THEN ST. FRANCIS

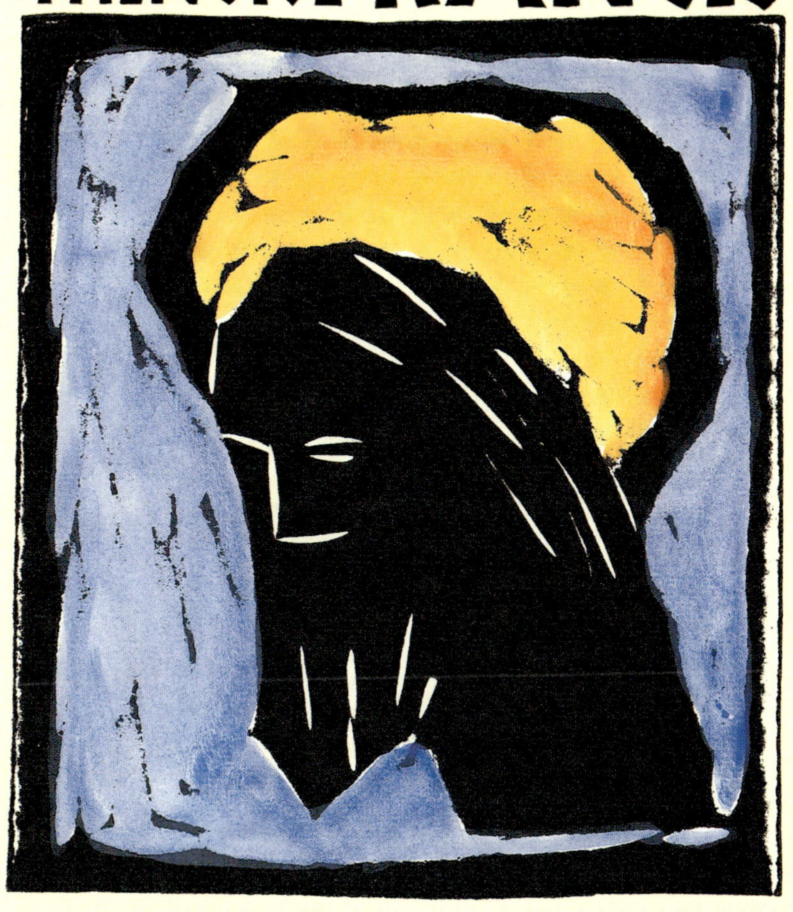

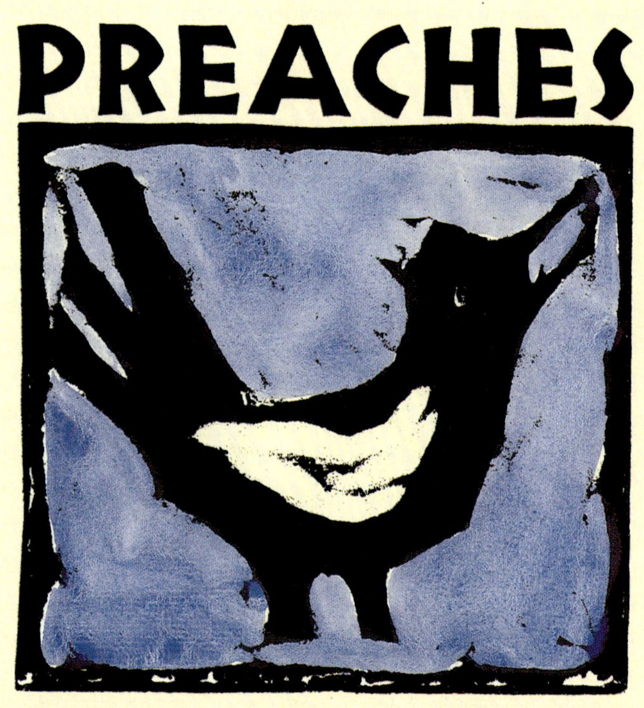
PREACHES

TO THE BIRDS

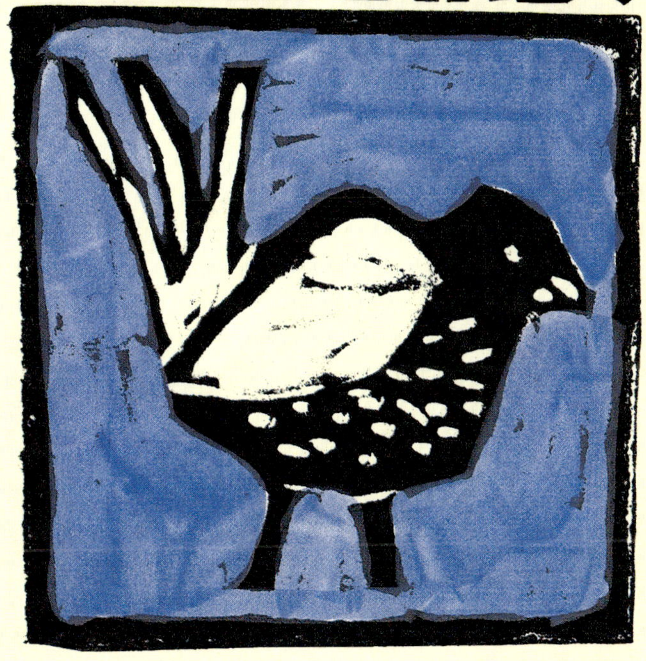

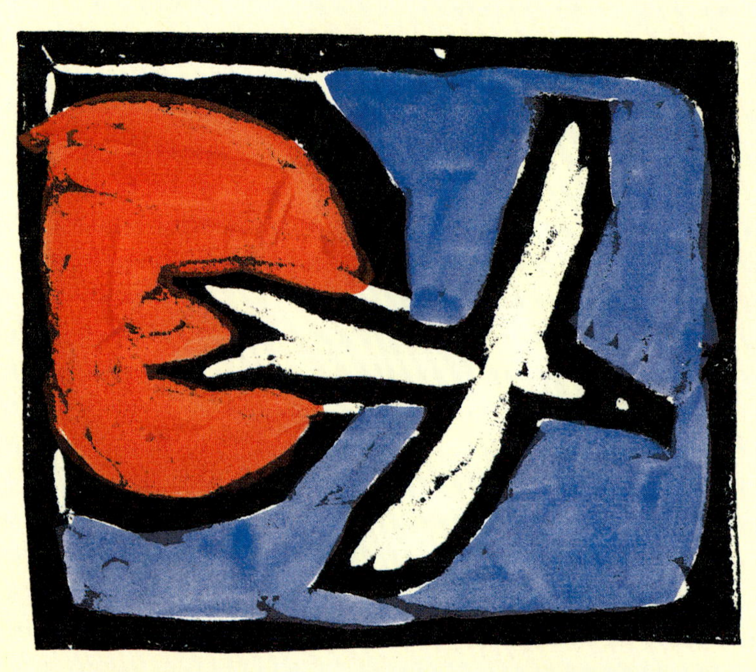

UNTIL THE SUN SETS

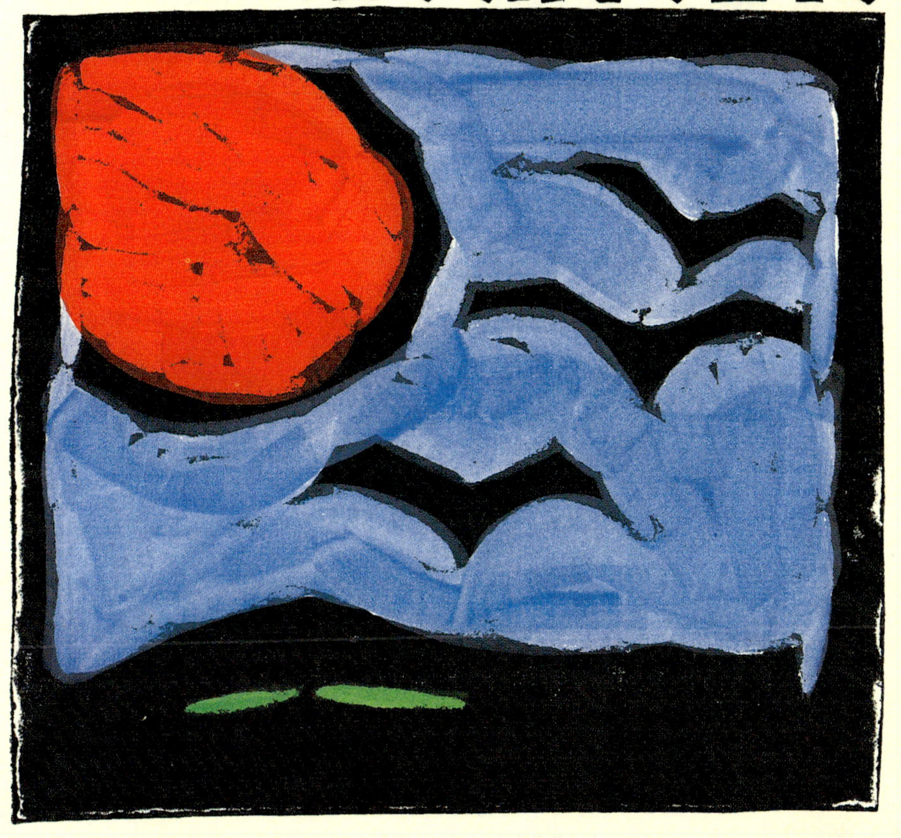

YES!

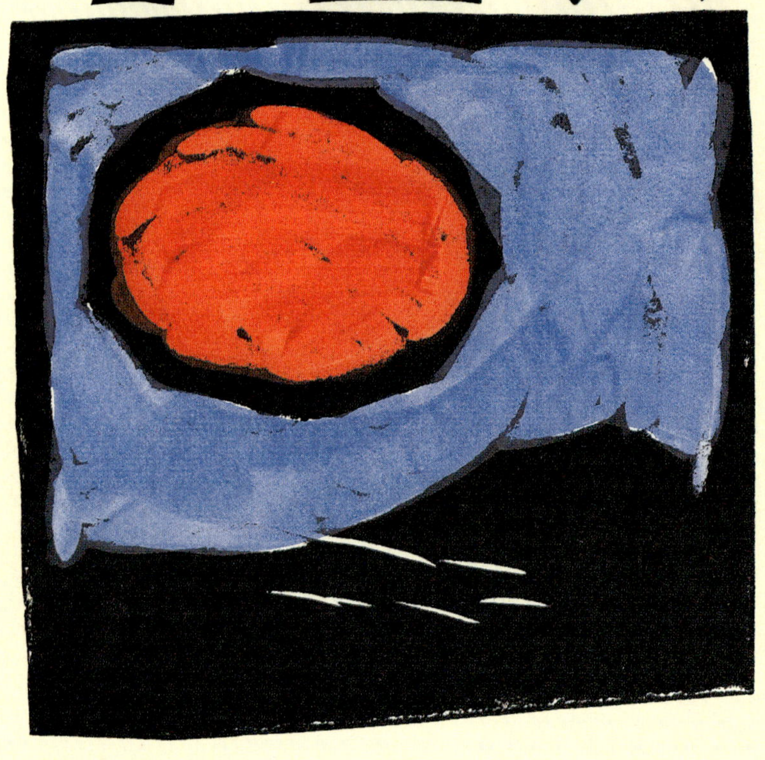

UNTIL THE SUN SETS

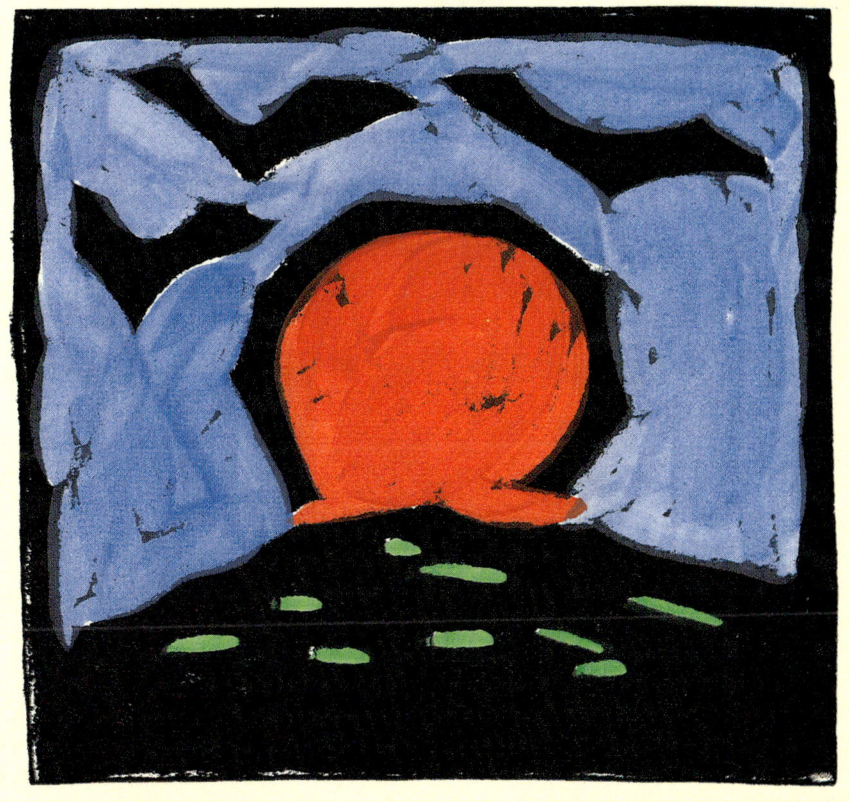

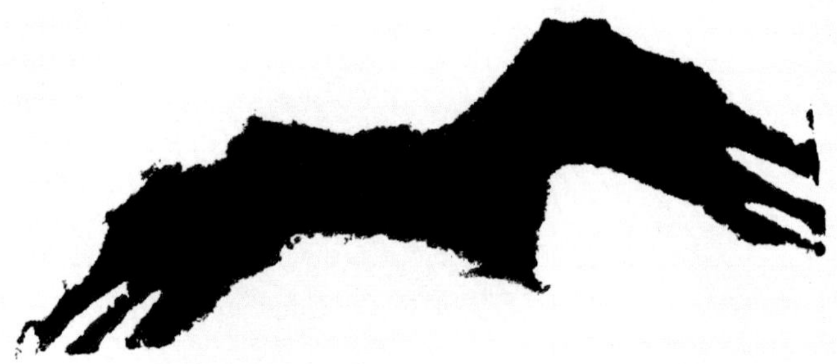

GOOD NIGHT

AFTERWORD

■ ■ ■

The original limited edition of *Saint Francis Preaches to the Birds* was a collaboration between Peter Schumann of Bread and Puppet Theater and Claire Van Vliet of the Janus Press. Schumann, who created the reliefs, is the founder of the Bread and Puppet Theater. Begun almost thirty years ago in New York's Lower East Side, the theater produced puppet shows on subjects ranging from fairy tales to the daily news. At the same time the theater expressed its involvement in contemporary social issues by creating rent-strike and voter-registration parades and demonstrations against the Vietnam War using over-life-sized puppets and masked performers. Since 1974, Bread and Puppet Theater has been located on a farm in Vermont, where a museum and various workshops and studios have been established. In addition to extensive international tours, the theater produces year-round puppet performances, which culminate each summer with *Our Domestic Resurrection Circus*. The concept of Bread and Puppet Theater performances derive from ancient folk traditions such as street carnivals, medieval morality plays, Sicilian puppetry, and Punch and Judy shows.

Claire Van Vliet is a printmaker; papermaker; and founder, in 1955, of the Janus Press. The press was established to print books and broadsides illustrated with original art: lithographs, relief etchings, woodcuts, and handmade paper imagery. Over ninety titles have been published by the Janus Press, most notably *The Tower of Babel*, *Aura*, *The Dream of the Dirty Woman*, *The Circus of Doctor Lao*, and *Aunt Sallie's Lament*. The press is located in northern Vermont, not far from the Bread and Puppet Theater, and has collaborated often with Peter Schumann. In 1989, Claire Van Vliet was the recipient of a MacArthur Fellowship in recognition of her original and innovative work in the book arts.

COLOPHON

■ ■ ■

The original limited edition of 100 copies of *Saint Francis Preaches to the Birds* was written by Peter Schumann and designed and printed by Claire Van Vliet at the Janus Press, Newark, Vermont, in 1978. The Masonite relief cuts were made by Peter Schumann and hand-colored by Solveig Schumann and Kaja McGowan. The text is set in Neuland, a cut letter designed to work with woodcuts for the Klingspor foundry in Offenbach, Germany, in 1923 by Rudolph Koch, who was their staff designer. In 1979, a small-format paper-pamphlet edition in black and white was issued, and in 1982, a second small-format paper-pamphlet edition with a solid blue sky was printed to celebrate the 800th anniversary of Saint Francis's birth.

Saint Francis of Assisi founded the Order of the Friars Minor (known as the Franciscans) in 1209. The story of Saint Francis preaching to the birds is apocryphal, but it clearly represents his special sympathy with the natural world and his respect for the spirituality of all living things.

Printed in Hong Kong.

Library of Congress Cataloging-in-Publication Data

Schumann, Peter, 1934–
St. Francis preaches to the birds / Peter Schumann.
p. cm.
Reprint. Originally published: Newark, Vt. : Janus Press, 1978.
ISBN 0-8118-0222-1
1. Schumann, Peter, 1934– 2. Francis, of Assisi, Saint, 1182–1226—Art. I. Title. II. Title: Saint Francis preaches to the birds.
NE539.S37A4 1992
769.92—dc20 92-7383
CIP

Distributed in Canada by Raincoast Books, 112 East Third Avenue, Vancouver, B.C. V5T 1C8

10 9 8 7 6 5 4 3 2 1

Chronicle Books
275 Fifth Street
San Francisco, California 94103